Bullfrog

by Jason Cooper

LG (K-3)
ATOS 3.7
0.5 pts
Non-Fiction

61579 EN

D0906525

BULLFROG

Life Cycles

Jason Cooper

Rourke
Publishing LLC
Vero Beach, Florida 32964

www.rourkepublishing.com

PHOTO CREDITS: Cover, p. 4, 15, 16, 18, 19 © Lynn M. Stone; p. 6 © Jerry Hennen; p. 7, 9, 10, 12, 13 © Breck Kent; p. 21 © Allen Sheldon.

Cover: *Beefy bullfrog is the largest of more than 20 kinds of true frogs in North America.*

Editor: Frank Sloan

Cover and page design by Nicola Stratford

Library of Congress Cataloging-in-Publication Data

Cooper, Jason, 1942-
  Bullfrog / Jason Cooper.
     p. cm. — (Life cycles)
Summary: Describes how bullfrogs reproduce and the changes that take place as one grows from egg to tadpole to adult frog.
Includes bibliographical references (p.   ).
  ISBN 1-58952-353-9 (hardcover)
  1. Bullfrog—Juvenile literature. [1. Bullfrog. 2. Frogs.] 1. Title.
  QL668.E27 C66 2002
  597.8'9—dc21

                                                        2002006227

Printed in the USA

CG/CG

Table of Contents

Bullfrogs like the quiet, weedy shores of ponds.

Music to Frogs

The story of the bullfrog begins with the sound of music. On warm summer nights, male bullfrogs along pond shores call *brr-rr-rr-um*, *brr-rr-rr-um*. That may not sound like music to you, but female bullfrogs love it.

Laying Eggs

When a female bullfrog joins a calling male, she is ready to lay eggs. While she lays her eggs, the male bullfrog **fertilizes** them. That makes the eggs **fertile**, so that they will hatch.

Frogs' eggs are spread over the surface of a marsh pool.

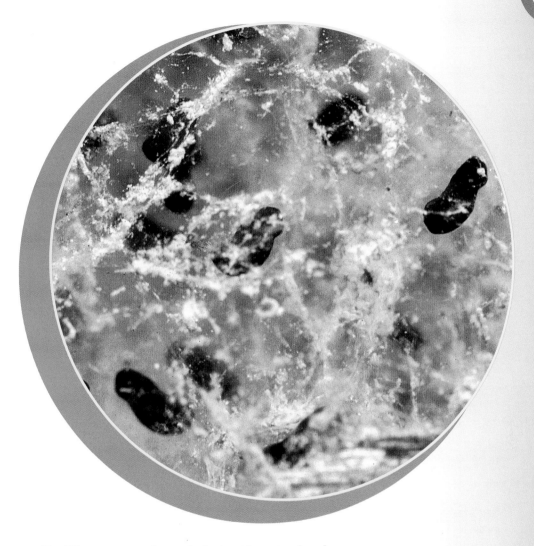

Bullfrog eggs hatch into tiny tadpoles.

The female lays from 5,000 to 20,000 eggs. They float in a thin, jelly-like layer on a pond surface. The whole egg mass may be more than 3 feet (1 meter) in diameter! Baby bullfrogs hatch from the eggs within just three to six days.

Tiny tadpoles must live in water, like fish.

Tadpoles

Baby bullfrogs are called **tadpoles**. They look and act far more like fish than frogs. For the first few weeks of life, a tadpole has a tail but no legs. Their tail movements allow tadpoles to swim.

Like other **amphibians**, bullfrogs are animals of land and water. During the egg and tadpole stages of life, however, bullfrogs live only in water, like fish. Tadpoles eat bits of **algae** and water plants. They also swim to the pond bottom to feed on dead animals.

Mostly tail, a tadpole looking for food visits the pond bottom.

A Deep Sleep

Tadpoles spend their first winter **hibernating** in the mud of the pond bottom. Hibernation is a period of deep sleep. Adult bullfrogs also hibernate in the pond mud.

Little Frogs

During their first summer, tadpoles sprout the beginnings of legs. During their second summer, many tadpoles turn into little frogs, or froglets.

This bullfrog tadpole has just begun to grow its front legs.

A tadpole with four legs begins to look more and more like a frog.

Some tadpoles don't change fully into frogs until their third summer.

As a tadpole grows, it spends more time at the edge or surface of the pond.

As amphibians, adult frogs can live on land or in the water.

Tadpole to Frog

The frog's body grows bigger and the tail grows smaller. Soon the tail disappears and becomes part of the frog's body. The legs grow out. The frog's breathing system changes, too. Now the frog can come out of the water and breathe air. By the end of its third summer, it looks like an adult.

By the age of two to four years, bullfrogs seek mates.

Surviving

One bullfrog in a zoo lived to the age of 15. But most bullfrogs are eaten by **predators** long before that. Most don't live past the tadpole stage. Those that survive seek a mate when they're between two and four years old. By that time they have become adults.

Predator and Prey

An adult bullfrog is a predator because it eats other animals. Bullfrogs live largely on a diet of insects.

Bullfrogs eat insects, like the dragonflies that share weedy pond shores with them.

Bullfrogs are the largest frogs in North America. (The saucer shape to the right of the eye is the frog's ear).

A big bullfrog may be up to 8 inches (20 centimeters) long. It will eat any animal it can swallow. That could be a small turtle, duck, snake, frog, or mouse! By eating its **prey** the bullfrog gets the food it needs.

A green heron grabs a frog from the water's edge.

The Life Cycle Goes On

On the other hand, even adult bullfrogs become prey for fish, snakes, turtles, minks, otters, raccoons, cranes, and herons. When a bullfrog dies, it becomes food for another animal. Through predator and prey, the energy in food passes back and forth.

Stage 1: **The adult frog lays eggs on the surface of the water.**

Stage 2: **Bullfrogs' eggs hatch as tiny tadpoles, which live in water.**

Stage 3: **Tadpoles first grow tails and legs. Then they become tiny frogs.**

Stage 4: **The small frog becomes a fully grown bullfrog.**

Glossary

algae (AL jee) — any one of the plant-like life forms, including common seaweed

amphibians (am FIB ee unz) — any one of the group of cold-blooded animals with backbones, moist skin, and (for most) the ability to live in water and on land

fertile (FUR till) — able to grow into a new plant or animal

fertilizes (FUR tuh liez ez) — makes an egg, such as a bullfrog's, develop and grow into an animal

hibernating (HIGH bur nay ting) — being in a state of deep sleep, usually during the winter

predators (PRED uh terz) — animals that catch and eat other animals for food

prey (PRAY) — an animal that is eaten by another animal

tadpoles (TAD POHLZ) — baby frogs or toads in their fish-like stages

Index

Further Reading

Arnosky, Jim. *All About Frogs.* Scholastic, 2002
Pascoe, Elaine. *Tadpoles.* Gale Group, 1996

Websites to Visit

http://search.yahooligans.com/search/ligans?p=bullfrog
http://www.personal.psu.edu/users/e/r/erw132/

About the Author

Jason Cooper has written several children's books about a variety of topics for Rourke Publishing, including recent series *China Discovery* and *American Landmarks*. Cooper travels widely to gather information for his books. Two of his favorite travel destinations are Alaska and the Far East.